AF408408

Discovering the Treasure

I Am Loved

MARIANNE CHALK

Dedication

To my grandchildren and
great-grandchildren, that they
may know the love of Jesus Christ
and the amazing life He has
planned for them.

I believe that Jesus is the Son of God.

Jesus lived with His Father in heaven.
He was responsible for creating the world
and everything in it. Even though Jesus was God's Son,
He had great power.

Jesus loved me so much that
He decided to leave heaven and come
to earth as a human being.

In LOVE
Jesus did this for me!

Jesus is wonderful!

When Jesus lived on earth
He healed the sick;
He multiplied bread and fish because people were hungry;
He calmed storms;
He walked on water.
He showed everyone His Father's love.

In LOVE
Jesus shows me His nature.

Jesus became human so I could know the Father through Him.
He became human to sacrifice Himself to forgive all the
sins of the world.
He became human, died, and rose from the dead for me.
Now I have the privilege of becoming a child of God because
I believe in Jesus and what He did for me.

In LOVE
Jesus died for me.

After Jesus was raised from the dead,
God sent His Holy Spirit to be with me.
Because I believe Jesus is God's Son, the
Holy Spirit lives in me.
The Holy Spirit is one with my spirit,
the inner part of me.

In LOVE
God created me perfectly!

I know that I am a child of God because
the Spirit of His Son lives in me.
Now God is my Father too.
The Father loves me just like He loves Jesus!
Whenever I need help, I can go to the Father.

In LOVE
the Father made me His child.

Jesus possesses all wisdom and knowledge.

Because His Holy Spirit and my spirit are one,
I can benefit from all that He knows.
Jesus helps me to understand Him and the Father.
Jesus helps me to understand His word.

In LOVE
Jesus provides for me.

God gave me Jesus' Spirit to help me.
Now I can do all the things that God asks me to do.
Jesus strengthens me.

In LOVE
God equips me.

Jesus is very smart.

He boldly spoke words from God.

These truthful words are filled with power.

Now I am blessed by these powerful words.

They change me, helping me to be just like Jesus.

In LOVE

God gave me His word!

As a human being, there are times when I may fail.
But then I remember Jesus!
I remember that we are one and I go to Him for help.
He strengthens me.
He gives me wisdom.

In LOVE
Jesus is attentive to me.

As a human being, it is sometimes hard to be nice to others.
But then I remember Jesus!
Jesus is kind, gentle, and good.
I am one with Jesus, and just like Him in my spirit.
In my spirit, I know that I am kind, gentle, and good.
Jesus helps me to live from my spirit so I can be nice to others.

In LOVE

Jesus helps me to live like Him.

There are times when I struggle to be patient.
At times I am tempted to behave badly.
But then I remember Jesus!
Jesus is patient and has self-control.
Because my spirit and Jesus' Spirit are one,
I too have patience and self-control.

In LOVE
Jesus helps me to behave better.

There were times when Jesus struggled.

He struggled when many people wanted His attention.

They followed Him everywhere.

Jesus struggled when it was time to die on the cross.

He kept Himself strong by spending time with His Father.

Jesus shows me how to keep strong by doing the same thing.

In LOVE

Jesus teaches me what to do when I struggle.

Sometimes I get too busy to spend time with Jesus.
Then I look at the amazing life that Jesus lived.
I observe what was important to Him.
Spending time talking to His Father was important.
I learn from Jesus that this is important for me too.

In LOVE

Jesus shows me what is important.

Jesus loves me and I am not afraid.

I give Him all my worries and concerns.

He cares for me and watches over me.

Through Jesus, the Father has given me everything that I need.

In LOVE

Jesus cares for me.

Even when I make mistakes Jesus still loves me.

This is called grace;

Jesus loves me even when I don't deserve it!

There is nothing I can do to stop Jesus' love for me.

This kind of love is extraordinary!

Jesus' LOVE for me never changes!

About the Author

Acts 4:13, New King James Version states, "Now when they saw the boldness of Peter and John, and perceived that they were uneducated and untrained men, they marveled. And they realized that they had been with Jesus." This is the desire of Marianne Chalk. As an author and illustrator, she hopes readers will perceive her love for Jesus, and the inspiration of the Holy Spirit, as she shares what is on her heart.

Marianne's career has been a journey of stepping stones that have led her to this moment in life. She is a retired RN with a BS in Counseling from Old Dominion University. It was the counseling degree that caused her career direction to shift to the criminal justice system. She provided parenting education to individuals who were court-ordered for child abuse issues. Then she volunteered to teach Bible study to incarcerated women for several years. Discovering there were no reentry programs available, with the help of other community volunteers, Marianne developed a faith-based nonprofit program for men and women released from jail. She wore many hats in the program including director, case manager, and fund-raiser.

In what seemed to be a strange twist, Marianne retired from reentry assistance believing the Lord was leading her and her husband Sam to purchase a bed and breakfast in western New York. Marianne and Sam had desired to be innkeepers for many years. Upon seeking guidance from the Lord, the dream of owning a bed and breakfast became a reality. Perhaps this part of her journey will be the next book!

Presently, Marianne's focus is sharing God's Word. She accomplishes this goal by teaching at her church, leading women's Bible study, and through her website Jesuscapturedmygaze.com, which she invites everyone to visit. The weekly post encourages the reader to be inspired by the Word of God. The artwork on the website is her creations.

Marianne and Sam live in Chesapeake, Virginia, and are blessed with three daughters, six grandchildren, and five great-grandchildren.